THE ROCKY ROAD OF GRIEF

Navigating the Journey into the Unknown

Sylvia Bryden-Stock

Author's Tranquility Press
ATLANTA, GEORGIA

Copyright © 2024 by Sylvia Bryden-Stock

All rights reserved. No part of this publication may be reproduced, distributed or transmitted in any form or by any means, including photocopying, recording, or other electronic or mechanical methods, without the prior written permission of the publisher, except in the case of brief quotations embodied in critical reviews and certain other noncommercial uses permitted by copyright law. For permission requests, write to the publisher, addressed "Attention: Permissions Coordinator," at the address below.

Sylvia Bryden-Stock/Author's Tranquility Press
3900 N Commerce Dr. Suite 300 #1255
Atlanta, GA 30344, USA
www.authorstranquilitypress.com

Ordering Information:
Quantity sales. Special discounts are available on quantity purchases by corporations, associations, and others. For details, contact the "Special Sales Department" at the address above.

The Rocky Road of Grief: Navigating the Journey into the Unknown / Sylvia Bryden-Stock
Paperback: 978-1-965463-95-6
eBook: 978-1-965463-02-4

DEDICATION

This book is dedicated to: All those who have been there during my own grief journey.

Especially my church family and my dear sister who listened and showed unconditional support. Also, the Princess Christian Care Home who selflessly supported through the latter stages of my husband's Young Onset Alzheimer's Disease and beyond.

I am also grateful for the power of scriptures to help me lean on the creator I believe in and bring ongoing inner peace during challenging times.

Contents

1 WHAT IS GRIEF? 1

2 WHY SHOULD WE GRIEVE? 5

3 MYTHS AROUND GRIEVING 10

4 A PERSONAL STORY 21

5 THE UNIQUENESS OF GRIEF 27

6 THE EMOTIONAL ROLLER COASTER OF GRIEF 31

7 GRIEF AND PHYSICAL HEALTH 36

8 HOW LONG SHOULD WE GRIEVE FOR? 41

9 GRIEF AND DREAMS 46

10 FINDING A PURPOSE AMONGST THE GRIEF 52

11 COMFORTING WORDS FOR THE GRIEVING HEART 57

FOREWORD

Grief is a Rocky Road

The grief journey is not a straight path. It is not a superhighway with a few rest stops along the way.

There is no precise road map. There are no checklists. There is no rubric for what to do, when, and how.

There are no linear, tight, predictable stages.

Grief refuses to be boxed.

Grief is a matter of the heart.

Our hearts have been hit. Our emotions are all over the place. Our minds spin. Our bodies tremble and our health can be affected. Our souls wince. Our relationships are shaken. Our future has been altered.

The sheer amount of change is stunning. One loss seems to lead to another. The ripple effects go on and on. We're weary. Exhausted. Broken. Shattered.

We get up and go through the motions. Nothing feels right. Everything is surreal. The world looks the same, but we know that everything has changed for us.

We wonder who we are now. We wonder what life is and what it will be. We wonder about, well, everything.

On top of all this, we feel lonely. We are individuals. Our hearts are unique. Our lives are unique. Our relationships and losses are unique. Grief is a lonely process.

Yes, this is a rocky road.

How do we do this?

In *The Rocky Road of Grief,* my friend Sylvia writes from a lifetime of experience with loss and grief. She knows this road all too well. She understands the twists, turns, and challenges of this arduous journey. She writes from personal and professional experience in grappling with the tough, heart-wrenching issues that arise from the death of a loved one.

Though grief is a lonely, individual process, we do not walk alone. There are many of us on this grief road. Though our hearts and experiences are different, we can walk together.

That's what Sylvia does in this book. Consider her one of your grief walking companions. She wants to meet you in the pages ahead and walk with you wherever you are in whatever you're going through.

Most importantly, Sylvia knows that Jesus is the ultimate grief companion. She knows Him well. She walks with Him. He is on this road with us. He is our Guide, our Counselor, our life.

You are not alone, though many times you will feel like you are.

You are not crazy, though at times you might wonder if you're losing your mind.

You will get through this, though at times you will wonder how.

The rocky road of grief is a one-step-at-a-time journey. Breathe deeply. Be kind to yourself. Be patient with yourself. This is hard.

Take a moment. Sit quietly. Listen. The Lord is here. Give yourself and this grief journey into the hands of Jesus. He knows it all. He knows you.

When you're ready, turn the page and join Sylvia on the rocky road of grief - one step, one page at a time.

Gary Roe
Amazon Bestselling Author, Speaker, and Grief Specialist

INTRODUCTION

There are many words that are used to define grief. In Miriam Websters Thesaurus grief is defined as deep sadness especially for the loss of someone or something loved. e.g. even the gruff grandfather felt a heartbreaking grief when the family dog died

When we think of grief what comes instantly to mind? The death of a loved one or a close friend.

How long should we grieve? It would be interesting to take a poll on this one!

There are many perceptions of

- how we should grieve
- when we should cease grieving
- what we should grieve.

Can we avoid grieving? What are the consequences of that?

Then, to be considered, are the different ways in which grief is expressed in different cultures which should be honoured and respected.

Many will struggle with what happens after the physical body has ceased existence which can deeply impact on the grieving journey depending on religious, spiritual and philosophical beliefs.

Trying to put grief into a logical box is impossible. Rather it is like trying to unravel a really messed up ball of wool.

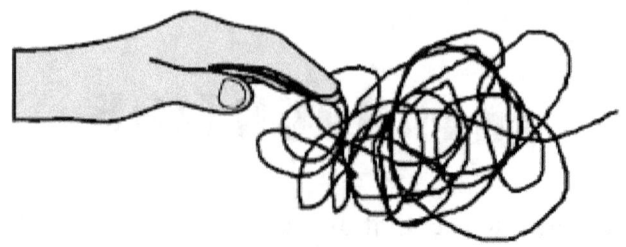

Everyone's ball of grief will look different, and the complexity vary with each individual.

Grief can also be like journeying through a maze and trying to find the way through to the "real" world.

In the UK we have a famous maze at Hampton Court Palace which is fun but challenging as you find yourself stuck in a corner when thinking you had found the way through!

Grief is a bit like navigating a maze of emotions and puzzling times as you struggle on.

This book is designed to help you navigate the grief journey and unravel your emotional grief ball.

You will realise that there is not a set pattern to follow.

- There are no defined rules to heed to
- There is no defined time to navigate grief. – BUT,
- You can and will survive and adjust in your own way and timing.

God saw him getting tired,
And a cure was not to be.
He wrapped him in his loving arms
And whispered "Come with Me"

He suffered much in silence,
His spirit did not bend.
He faced his pain with courage, until the very end.

He tried so hard to stay with us,
But his fight was not in vain,
God took him to His loving home,
And freed him from his pain.

CHAPTER 1
WHAT IS GRIEF?

Recently I began a grief support group at my local church for those having challenges with life, causing them to experience grief. Interestingly, when chatting with members of the congregation the association of grief seemed only to be associated with the death of a loved one.

Reflecting on the definition from Marriam Webster quoted in the introduction, it seems clear that many things that happen to us in life can cause us to grieve.

Think back to childhood for a moment. Suddenly, you wake up one morning, have a hasty breakfast, then off you go to be dropped off at nursery. Both you and parent express grief from being separated. In time you adjust but initially it is very traumatic.

What about that first day at school?

When growing up, I did not have the blessing of dealing with separation grief and learning socialising skills. Mummy and I were suddenly faced with a whole new way of life Monday to Friday each week. I cried a lot on day one while mother was back home worried about how I was adjusting to school life. Yes, adjustment did take place as I would proudly announce that the teacher was always right, and parents knew nothing!

Grief is associated with loss of something or someone. I have witnessed children and adults sobbing over the death of a hamster or budgerigar. Only very small pets, but who have become part of the family.

Grief is very much a part of this earthly life journey, especially at this time of uncertainty and unrest. Nothing feels secure anymore.

There is an underlying fear and worry around day-to-day existence. It is almost as if there is sense of constant grief concerning "this could happen with my health" or "is my job stable?" or "will I be able to meet my bill payments?"

Since the COVID Pandemic our lives have never really been the same. It's as if we are living in a new norm.

Many have lost their employment, businesses have gone bankrupt.

Family tensions at an all-time high as they struggle to make ends meet.

Mental Health statistics and suicide rates have soared and there is a definite sense of uncertainty in our world.

Our hearts are broken almost daily over the news and social media posts that seemingly only want to tell us negative news and therefore increase to stress us out and keep us in fear.

Grief in our modern world has a whole new look to it.

My neighbour recently came to tell me her husband had lost his wallet while out to lunch with a colleague. All his credit and debit cards were in it along with his senior rail card and free bus pass for seniors. In this fast-paced world, understandably he was devastated and grieving the possible outcome if someone got hold of his bank cards etc. They were visibly grieving this experience.

Imagine having an important hospital appointment deferred when in constant pain or turning up for scheduled day surgery, only to be told they have had to cancel it?

I could go on and on! Suffice it to say that all sudden change in circumstances has the potential to have an initial emotional response which is a way of expressing the grief reaction to what has occurred.

Reactions such as– Tears, anger. Feelings of uncertainty, blame, panic, impulse action due to an adrenaline "fight or flight" response.

In the western world we tend to hide our grief or not see life experiences that upset us as a grieving time.

I am a firm believer that grief should not be associated only with physical death, but with other disturbing circumstances as well.

We desire life to be a smooth ride, without any ups and downs. Without challenges we would become overly complacent and probably bored. Challenges are there to help us grow in character.

Acknowledging this, plus the associated grief aspect can aid adjustment and recovery. Also, emotional response skills gained to help with future life hiccups when they arise – because they surely will, in a variety of ways.

Let's not forget those moments where we can grieve with someone else as they go through their own traumatic experience.

As someone who believes in the power of Jesus to help us with grief, He told us in scripture that we would have tribulation is this fallen world, but he also promised his peace to help us in times of grief. (John 16 v 33, John 14 v 27).

So, we could say therefore, that grief is part of life, and we need strategies to help us grieve positively and move forward into a new way of life.

So what emotions are in this ball of grief I talked about?

How do we navigate from loss to remaking life?

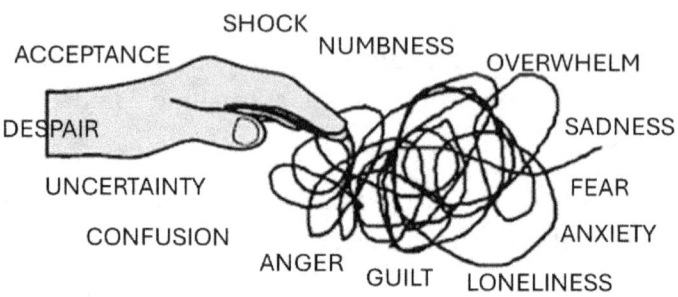

One is struggling to find a way to accept a new way of life, while unravelling the mix of emotions that express themselves along the way.

Grief is not a definitive start and finish.

Depending on who or what you are grieving it is more about adjustment as life moves forward to a different expression.

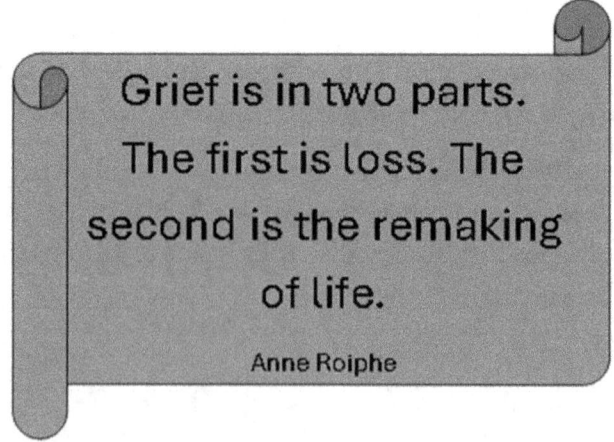

Grief is in two parts. The first is loss. The second is the remaking of life.

Anne Roiphe

CHAPTER 2
WHY SHOULD WE GRIEVE?

The best way to heal from any form of loss is to allow yourself to grieve.

It is the best way to adjust to a new way of life without a person or circumstance you have suddenly had thrust in front of you. Learning to adjust to a new norm.

Sometimes a loss has an amazing purpose locked in it. For example, you may be grieving a job loss not knowing that a better job offer is waiting in the wings for you.

It is not cowardly to express grief. It takes courage to express the feelings you are experiencing after a loss. The thought of fully feeling the pain is heart wrenching. Best to "keep doing!" to avoid what needs to be poured out from within.

How often do you avoid facing up to a painful situation in life?

I recall a situation in a work management position where there was jealousy involved. To keep it short, I was wrongly accused of abusing funds and investigated by senior management. They suspended me and I became stressed and anxious about writing a statement following clever questioning to confuse me as they interrogated me. I kept putting off the moment until a counsellor told me to go home and get my statement written. When I faced up to the task, relief and inner peace arose within me as they decided to pay me to leave. A meeting with a new senior manager before I left looked at the evidential file and said should never have happened and promised a fair reference for future employment. I learned a big lesson regarding facing challenges head on and walking through the "dark valley".

I think of that favourite Psalm of David in the Bible which says -

...

Yea, though I walk through the valley of the shadow of death, I will fear no evil; For You are with me;

Notice he talks of going **through** the valley which means there is a time when the dark valley fades plus there is a God who will walk the dark valley with him.

Grief is a new and dark valley journey that cannot be avoided but being a believer in a God who wants to walk with us through life, Psalm 23 is a comfort; knowing we do not have to be alone when dealing with any loss in life.

A tunnel has an entrance and exit. In the middle is the darkest place and illustrates the darkness of the grief journey. Let's hang on to the knowledge that there is light at the end of the tunnel.

THE ROCKY ROAD OF GRIEF

As time passes mini tunnels may loom up in front of you as memories trigger those grief emotions again. All part of the ongoing new way of life. They will become shorter and more easily navigated.

When we allow ourselves to grieve, we are giving our whole being a road map to navigate the future in a way that allows adjustment to the loss we are encountering.

Allowing for that brain fog to clear over time and being able to have more clarity and focus with day-to-day living.

Sometimes, not knowing how you are going to survive following the traumatic situation you are dealing with creates fear and anxiety.

Facing a new day almost paralyses you. Staying under the bed clothes seems the best option.

At some point the feelings associated with loss need to be expressed, facilitating a life balanced with moving forward but not denying the pain.

How you express your own grief will vary. We all grieve in ways that are unique to us. It is not for anyone to judge or think that you should follow their chosen recipe for handling grief.

It's like going for meal with friends and one of the party insists that their menu choice is definitely the best option, expecting everyone to fall in line with them.

We are all uniquely created by God and meant to express that uniqueness in all life experiences – including grief.

There are many organisations that offer support during times of grief, whatever you are grieving but along with the guidance they give, it is known that people express and handle grief within their overall make-up.

What is emphasised is the importance of expressing grief to prevent longer term issues cropping up such as emotional, mental, physical symptoms that are puzzling. Ultimately, they stem from not allowing grief to be dealt with in a healthy way.

During my nursing career I spent several years as a community nursing sister and came in contact with many grieving patients – all manifesting their grief very differently. That was when grief following the death of a loved one was acknowledged with the wearing of a black arm band for around six months or dressing in black for the same period. Folks would be reminded that any strange behaviour traits or change in verbal communication would be because they were grieving.

Other painful situations were expected to have the good old British "stiff upper lip" approach which was how we dealt with the second world war.

I recall one lady I visited whose husband had passed away some years before. Her way of grieving was quite unique as I was about to find out. I went to sit down at the dining room table oblivious to the jacket and cap adorning it. There may even have been a pair of shoes beneath as well! "Don't you sit on that chair nurse!" she roared at me "That's Charlies chair!" She obviously spoke to Charlie frequently imagining him sitting there. Dutifully I removed myself and apologised. For sure, she was not avoiding dealing with her grief!

Thankfully now there is so much information available online regarding grief and many support organisations exist to help deal with grief for all areas that generate the emotions of grief – see UK resources at the end of this book.

Let's not forget other things that occur in life that we grieve over or, should allow the pain to be expressed in a positive way that strengthens the resolve to move forward without regret or guilt e.g.

- First day at School/Nursery
- First Haircut affecting hairdressing visits throughout life. (I love going to have my hair done!)
- First visit to the Doctor/Dentist
- Death of one's favourite pet
- Miscarriage or Abortion
- A painful divorce
- Sudden job loss

And the list could go on.

It seems very clear that grief is a part of life and should not be avoided but expressed in one's own unique way, allowing for ongoing adjustment to a new way of life.

CHAPTER 3
MYTHS AROUND GRIEVING

> Grief is tidal. In time, it can recede and leave us with feelings of peace and advancement, only for it to wash back in with all its crushing hopelessness and sorrow. Back and forth it goes, but with each retreating drift of despair, we are left a little stronger, more resilient, more essential and better at our new life.
>
> – *Nick Cave*

It is interesting how many different theories there are around how the grief journey does and should pan out.

When you are going through a time of grieving a loved one or any other form of grief, do you find that folks around you want to offer a set pattern or strategy saying thigs like –

- I understand how you feel. In reality they have no idea

exactly how you feel
- If I were you... They are not you. You are on your own unique journey.

Let's take a look at some myths around grieving. The ten most popular –

Myth Number One

Everyone goes through grief stages. It's like there are a set of rules to follow to cope with grief.

The fact is – there are no hard and fast ways in which you should express grief.

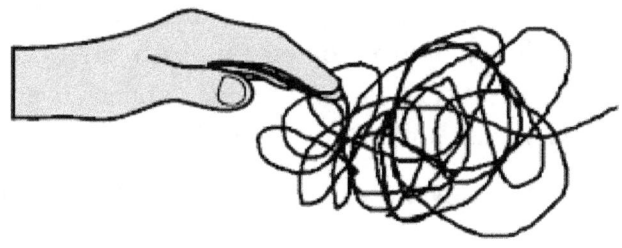

In the introduction I wrote that grieving was like unravelling a ball of mixed emotions. That is more likely what happens with any form of grief.

It has been accepted in many cases that grief was about a linear journey of five stages consisting of - grief: *denial, anger, bargaining, depression and acceptance.*

This comes from a book by Elizabeth Kubler-Ross written in 1968 for hospice patients preparing to die and is unrelated to other grief encounters.

Myth Number Two

Grief and Mourning are the same thing -

Grief causes many different behaviours to manifest, one of these being mourning.

Knowing that grief is concerned with the loss of something or someone, we can mourn many losses during life's journey, that when it is the loss of a loved one from death, grief causes many emotions to arise such as numbness, anger, overwhelming emotional pain, guilt and more.

Mourning is the way we express our grief to the world. For example –

- Wearing black clothes for a period of time or a black armband
- Wring out the emotions of grief in a journal
- Using cultural rituals to express grief

Research studies show some common emotions associated with major losses –

- **Numbness** – feeling no emotions during the first few days of traumatic loss.
- **Pining** – especially the loss of someone dear to you and desperately wishing them to be around…

- **Despair and confusion** - manifesting as anger or guilt
- **Recovery** - where adjustment to a way of living with the loss and allowing life to move forward.

Let's remember that these are just an illustration of grief expression.

Mourning is the expression of the mix of emotions that churn around and can rise up to be expressed at any moment.

Mourning is the way emotions are acted out to allow adjustment and a way to live alongside the deep grief.

Myth Number Three

Women grieve more than men -

The truth is that all people grieve differently and unique to who they are.

Because of the different way that men and women view the world, this can spill over into processing grief.

Men are more logical in their world view and may want to view grief as an experience that fits into the "Fix it" mould, not understanding why they can't. Maybe they have been taught that men don't cry from a young age. Women may more easily cry and overtly express their grief: although many women have stated they are unable to cry.

Men and women will grieve in their own way but will ultimately express a typical grief journey.

Myth Number Four

If you are not crying, you are not grieving –

Grief is expressed in many ways and crying is one of them.

Sometimes one can cry tears of joy as well as sorrow. Some people can deeply feel grief without shedding a single tear. The male species are especially not supposed cry but show strength and support whilst keeping emotions deep within themselves.

Cultures differ and with some crying and loud wailing is expected for days and weeks following their loss of a loved one by death.

The emotions expressed during grief are many and not crying does not indicate that there is no feeling of sadness.

Many who grieve experiences related to their work environment can often hold it within themselves.

Having had a nursing background and seen some terrible circumstances I had to learn to hold back my emotional response to dealing with what was happening.

Whether you are someone who very easily cries for joy or grief, or somebody who does not shed a tear, grief will be expressed in a way unique to you.

When my father died I was devastated and wept bitterly while mother, as was her make-up, did not overtly show her grief.

Myth Number Five

Ignoring your pain will make it go away –

Ignoring or denying your pain whatever you are grieving is only a temporary solution.

Like physical pain from an injury that needs acknowledgement and being helped to heal, the same goes for emotional pain – the pain of grief. Like ignored physical pain, grief pain ignored is not going to aid true healing. "Diversional Therapy" from either drugs or overactive "busyness" will eventually come to ahead and have to be faced.

Read the chapter that speaks of the physical effects of grief coming later. Facing up to any kind of loss will enable strategies for coping and adjusting to a "new normal". This, in terms of loss of a loved one means gradually becoming OK with alone time to reflect and enjoy past memories and recover from those guilt and anger emotions and other grief manifestations.

Myth Number Six

The first year is the hardest –

Grief is not easy to live with –it is a tough roller coaster ride.

There is no time limit on dealing with grief. There is no specific recipe for handling grief. The emotional ingredients of grief are not like mixing a set of ingredients, cooking them, and out comes a perfect result every time. People may use the same set of ingredients and put them together very differently for their own best result. Grief ingredients are not put in a standard, one size fits all pot. The mix of emotional trauma ingredients are unique to you and "cooked" in line with how you view life and it's challenges. It's like having a bag of ingredients thrown at you that you have never used before and then doing your best to make something out of them.

Many folks will say that the pain of loss increases as reality embeds itself. Pain can rise up at any time even years on. You hear a song, a favourite hymn is sung in church, someone says something in conversation for example and painful memories are triggered.

That phrase "well now, you've got through the first year!" So what?!

Myth Number Seven

Grief gets better over time -

There is no set time for adjusting to a new way of life.

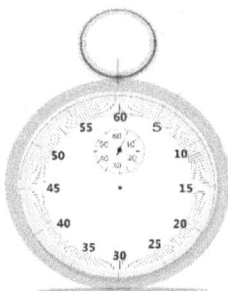

There was a saying – "Time heals all wounds" and can be associated with circumstantial grief but less likely with the loss through death of someone dear to you.

Acute grief of a loved one passing may ease over time but will not disappear entirely. You cannot get to a point where they are no longer a part of you. Their love remains in your heart always, and missing their physical presence will take some major adjusting to over time. This can vary from person to person as feelings of guilt, remorse, anger, frustration over day-to-day tasks you now must learn for yourself. A few of the emotions around your grief journey.

Myth Number Eight

Grief has an end point –

When grief hits it is not like beginning a race of sprint or even a marathon that has a finishing point.

You may well wish the turmoil of emotions to suddenly disappear and total 24/7 peace and joy to burst forth like a champagne cork pop from the bottle.

Even those with a deep faith in God and a knowledge of the spirit self being alive in a new body in heaven who you will see again one day, still miss the physical presence and have days of emotional struggle. External reminders can cause grief to emerge again at any moment.

Myth Number Nine

Grief has a point of closure to be achieved –

Getting to the point of some kind of closure with grief is important but this does not fully close the book on grief.

Grief is not something that will go away. Don't get hung up on the "get over it" trap. Though you may wish to be free of all the emotions and physical effects it causes, it is something that intertwines with your ongoing life without the loved one so dear to you. Time may have moved on, and life is becoming more manageable when you could be anywhere, and something triggers memories – even happy ones can resurrect pangs of grief. Make sure you have non-judgmental, supportive friends you can turn to.

It is important to be aware of the negative and painful attitudes around grief; including the myth that grief has an end point.

Myth Number Ten

Grieving people just need to get over it -

You do move on in life from grief but will never get over it.

Some people will always talk about grief with "getting over it" and nothing is further from the truth. A better phrase is that you will "get on with it". The get over it myth stated so often probably is triggered from the person's own way of dealing with grief. Perhaps they have never faced a deep and painful loss and do not know what to say.

Take comfort in the following poem -

SYLVIA BRYDEN-STOCK

If Tears Could Build A Stairway

If tears could build a stairway
And memories were a lane
We would walk right up to Heaven
And bring you back again

No farewell words were spoken
No time to say goodbye
You were gone before we knew it
And only God knows why

Our hearts still ache in sadness
And secret tears still flow
What it meant to lose you
No one will ever know

But now we know you want us
To mourn for you no more
To remember all the happy times
Life still has much in store

Since you'll never be forgotten
We pledge to you today
A hallowed place within our hearts
Is where you'll always stay

-Author Unknown

CHAPTER 4
A PERSONAL STORY

Grief can strike in many ways. It may be a sudden event that occurs like an uncle of mine who left for work and never returned. He had a heart attack on the way to work and my aunt received the news from a policeman knocking on her door.

Someone could go to work and be told they are being made redundant and have to pack up their things and leave.

Then there are those who find themselves on a challenging sickness journey with their loved one, watching them progress slowly towards physically leaving this world.

That was my experience with my dear husband who was diagnosed with Young Onset Alzheimer's Disease.

With any form of dementia, one is watching a person gradually disappear from you. With the manifestation of the disease over many years they are dying a little each day.

That was my personal journey of ongoing grief as my man slowly progressed with the awful disease.

Watching his ongoing suffering-

- The frustration as day-to-day tasks became more and

more difficult.
- The challenge of communication skills resulting in angry outbursts.
- My agony as I witnessed the decline of his control of bodily elimination functions which he was aware of, one day he stated on my arrival at the Care Home "I think I am losing it down there."

The emotional turmoil of grieving each new phase of deterioration sure took its toll.

A journey of continual acknowledgement, adjustment and acceptance with each new manifestation of behaviour and loss of bodily functions etc.

I had a plan devised for the way we would walk this unknown future based on my nursing and dementia care background. It was to complete it all at home.

Facing up to his having to partake in 24/7 care in a Dementia Care Home was a major hurdle as I felt like my soul had been ripped out the day he never returned from day care, due to behaviour traits plus sleepless nights for nearly three years. The deep inner pain of loss of his presence at home. Even letting go of doing his laundry was so painful.

Then there were the times that he seemed to be rapidly slipping away and I was preparing for him to leave this world and suddenly he bounced back.

I was fully experiencing the emotional roller coaster of caring as I clung tightly to my trust in God and his promise of peace in the bible –

"My peace I leave with you; My peace I leave with you. Not as the world gives give I unto you. Ley not your heart be troubled, neither let it be afraid." John chapter 14 verse 27

THE ROCKY ROAD OF GRIEF

Repeated chest infections occurred towards the end, and I was told that further antibiotics would not work, and all medication was stopped.

Now the end was definitely close and two weeks of 24/7 daily support with trusty sister and dear friend began as we stayed with him and took turns for rest overnight in a bedroom provided by the staff on his unit.

We watched as he took his last breath and took leave of his physical body and moved on to be with Jesus. My faith believes in heaven and I knew I would meet him again one day.

That knowledge created a sense of relief that earthly suffering was finally over, and I was on an emotional "high" throughout all the funeral arrangements and kicking off a Probate journey for house issues etc. until – Around five months following his transition I awoke one day to the full reality that I had to face. The earthly, human experience of grief.

Here I was, about to begin another roller coaster ride.

In life generally I have never enjoyed going on fairground rides – especially the huge roller coasters with the up, down, round and round, tossing and turning. I braved it once but throughout the whole ride was anxious and desperate to be able to get off!

Now I was beginning an emotional roller coaster of grief that did not fit a linear logical solution.

I had my own ball of tangled emotions to deal with.

As a dedicated follower of Jesus, who knew of many bible verses to cling to, I was challenged with the guilt associated with the knowledge of the joy of seeing him again with the pain in my heart as I faced each day.

The John 14 v 27 bible verse that was telling me not to let my heart be troubled seemed far out of reach.

Psalm 23 where we are assured that God is with us through the dark valley was not yet real to me.

Where is God in this dark valley of mine?

Where is his rod and staff to comfort me?

The powerful part that says we will go **through** the valley seemed inconceivable as I stepped onto this new roller coaster experience.

How must those who have no God to turn to cope with the despair and loneliness of suddenly being a "one" and no longer a "two" who had been through so much together and survived, as our love and God's power enabled us to survive?

If we are told in the book of Psalms by King David who suffered much during his life that "the joy of the Lord is my strength", where was my joy and His strength right now?

I was to see slowly, as I trusted my God and stayed in the knowledge that Jesus took all our pain and suffering to the cross, that because of a strong faith, I would get through the roller coaster ride and have a great purpose and passion for those who are grieving because "I have been there".

I heard all the classic phrases from the last chapter.

The one that stands out as I write is what I was told about six months after Brian's transition. "Life has to go on!" Sure, it does I remember thinking BUT it is going to be very different!

I have experienced that the "get the first year over …" encouragement does not necessarily apply. The roller coaster ride does become more adjusted to over time but, like life generally, is a journey of ups and downs.

In my book The Rocky Road to Peace of Mind, a final statement says, "True peace of mind means that we accept that on some days we may not have peace of mind".

One powerful tool that has always helped me through any of life's challenges, is to have an attitude of gratitude.

This can be key to surviving as you travel the grief train. Yes, grief is like boarding a train that is an all-stations stopper that represents different emotions.

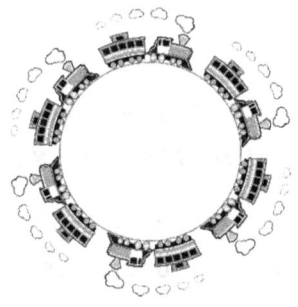

The train doesn't cease its journey but keeps moving, ever circulating through them all.

I had a choice – keep going through the tough times ahead or get off and become a victim and hang around at one stop or work through and adjust to a new way of living each day.

Even as I write this chapter some emotional pain is rising within again. This confirms for me that grief is part of our earthly life but can be lived with and the memories create empathy and understanding towards others who are grieving.

Also, my character is persevering and persistent in its make up. This has brought me through many challenges over the years as no matter what I will cling to the promises of God in the bible.

Psalm 23 is a powerful psalm so I will include it here for you –

The Lord is my shepherd; I shall not want.

2 He maketh me to lie down in green pastures: he leadeth me beside the still waters.

3 He restoreth my soul: he leadeth me in the paths of righteousness for his name's sake.

4 Yea, though I walk through the valley of the shadow of death, I will fear no evil: for thou art with me; thy rod and thy staff they comfort me.

5 Thou preparest a table before me in the presence of mine enemies: thou anointest my head with oil; my cup runneth over.

6 Surely goodness and mercy shall follow me all the days of my life: and I will dwell in the house of the Lord forever.

The greatest gift that has emerged from my grief journey is a passion to help others find inner peace in times of overwhelming sorrow and the storms of life. It makes everything that one went through make some sense.

> The climb might be tough and challenging, but the view is worth it. There is a purpose for that pain; you just can't always see it right away.
> -Victoria Arien

CHAPTER 5
THE UNIQUENESS OF GRIEF

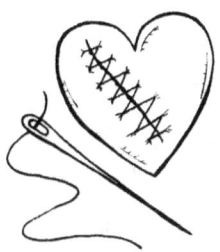

We often speak of things, or a person, being unique.

I decided to look up the root meaning of the word unique and found the following -

Unique comes originally from the Latin word '**unicus**' — meaning "only, single, alone of its kind".

Isn't that how we should look at the grief experience?

We are all created as a unique individual walking out our journey through life.

When grief comes knocking at the door, everyone's sudden exposure to something very different to what was the "norm" of life will be "alone of its kind".

Although we know that key emotions such as grief, numbness, anger, denial, anxiety, depression, are expressed as a new way of life is adjusted to, they are very singular to each individual.

In life generally we create patterns of coping with challenges in a way that works for us.

Dealing with grief is no different.

Some folks will overtly announce their anger using very expletive language!

Others hold anger deep inside and let it fester until it maybe manifests in physical health issues, or their very make-up seems to enable calmness throughout whatever life throws at them.

I have witnessed opposite poles of dealing with grief in my time. Neither to be judged in any way.

Number one – A friend of mine was bereaved at a fairly young age. Not long after her husband's passing, she answered an advertisement in the local paper (quite out of character) and decided to meet a widower for a coffee. Her strategy was to meet where she could drive past him and if he looked "suspect" to drive on and return home. They met and had coffee at a portacabin by the River Thames, chatting for a long while. Romance ensued and three years later they married, and joint families lived a happy life together.

Number Two – The passing of their spouse after being her carer for a number of years so deeply impacted that they became stuck in grief anguish for many years before actively engaging with others as time went on, being without their presence and the role they played in their marriage. Adjustment seemed almost unattainable as they plunged deeper and deeper into the pain within their heart.

I remember a TV programme here in the UK called Ready, Steady Cook. A number of ingredients were placed on the worktop for them to create within a set time scale. The finished dishes were very different and unique to each chef participating.

THE ROCKY ROAD OF GRIEF

Isn't grieving like that?

Common feelings include:

- sadness.
- shock.
- denial.
- numbness, a sense of unreality.
- anger.
- guilt.
- blame.
- relief.

However, no one person will express any of the above feelings listed, in the same way or at the same time.

I clearly recall a patient's wife when I was a community nurse who vehemently expressed anger and blame during the usual bereavement visit, we routinely carried out. Kindly showing empathy to her sudden loss of her husband the response was not as expected –

"Don't you feel sorry for me nurse! Look in that drawer over there! See that b……..cap? I bought him that last Christmas and he never b…….. wore it!".

Then there was another instance where it was some years since husband had died and a routine visit for her took place. The small dining room had a standard layout with dining chairs placed around. One had a gentlemen's jacket adorning it and a cap hanging on the back. n

I went to sit down to place her visit record ready for completing, when a voice roared at me *"Don't you sit their nurse, that's Charlie's chair!"*

Of course, I speedily moved chairs and apologized.

Here are two opposite grief expressions and ways of coping with their loss. Neither are right or wrong, just different ways of coping.

In its uniqueness, grief needs an unconditional, non-judgmental support approach. Not attempting to place individuals into the same puzzle box with a set way of putting pieces together.

If the same jigsaw puzzle was given to a number of people to complete, I am sure they will approach the completion differently – outside edge pieces meticulously set aside to be completed first; Outside edge and inner pieces jointly put together; segments of the picture put together and placed where they fit in the picture. They will all complete their puzzle but in a way that is unique to them.

Like the image at the beginning of the chapter, those grieving any life situation will have a way of mending the brokenness felt in their heart.

That is fine so long as the scar created allows for ongoing adjustment to a new way of living.

"She was no longer wrestling with the grief but could sit down with It as a lasting companion and make it a sharer in her thoughts."

-George Elliot

CHAPTER 6
THE EMOTIONAL ROLLER COASTER OF GRIEF

I was talking with someone recently about grief and life; they stated that grieving loss was also part of life and like anything else it is how we respond to it.

In many ways I agree with them, except to say that the loss of a loved one does have a special grief response compared to many of life's painful experiences.

When something or someone especially close to us is suddenly not there anymore, we travel a journey of very mixed emotions. I mentioned the roller coaster earlier but let's look at the ride in more depth.

There are some interesting articles (many of them!) online that gives tips on how to ride the roller coaster at a fairground. Here are some of the suggested tips I found –

1. Even though you hate roller coasters you can successfully endure the ride. Make sure that you

mentally gear up for the ride, choose a seat in the middle and check the restraints, and then hold on tight, take a deep breath, and enjoy the ride.
2. Learn a little about them before you ride.
3. Understand that roller coasters are meant to be scary.
4. Go with friends as they will comfort you and make you feel less scared.
5. Try to remember that the whole thing, for better or worse, will be over extremely quickly.
6. Follow the instructions of the park employees and the ride guidelines.
7. Resist the urge to close your eyes. Inexperienced riders often think that closing your eyes will help make it less scary and that you'll feel better,

There are more tips that are supposed to help make the ride become a totally pleasant experience, with a desire to ride more difficult ones!

Let's now compare them with the roller coaster ride of grief.

Take number 1, that tells us that by mentally gearing up for the ride you will successfully endure the ride.

Can we mentally gear up for the grief roller coaster? I think not. When a loss suddenly takes place there is no way one is ready for the ride ahead. Even if the ride begins following a diagnosis that will become terminal e.g. Dementia or Alzheimer's Disease or even cancer that is already pre-terminal.

You are suddenly strapped into your seat which is definitely not going to be "the ride of your life" in a positive way!

There is no step-by-step guidebook to follow. Remember the ball of wool that needs untangling? There are no defined ways to untangle the ball, of grief emotions.

THE ROCKY ROAD OF GRIEF

Number 2 is interesting. There is no well-defined, cast in stone way to tackle grief emotions. As has been talked about earlier.

Number 3 -has some truth for those thrust into grieving – especially a loved one or someone you are closely connected to. Facing a totally different way of life is scary. We have to navigate the journey within the uniqueness of who you are.

Number 4 – A grieving heart too needs comfort and support from friends and others. Maybe a support group. Someone who supports unconditionally without trying to "fix" everything or suggesting defined steps to moving forward. There may be others who have walked the path you are now thrust on to who, by sharing their experience, can be reassuring for you.

Number 5 – The grief roller coaster ride is in no way comparable to a fair ground ride. It is definitely not over quickly! It is an ongoing battle of emotions as adjustment to a new way of life is thrust upon you.

Number 6 – Are there clear-cut instructions to the emotional roller coaster ride? There are those that believe in a linear journey from one emotion to another and then you reach acceptance. Grief is not like a factory production line where one component is completed and then another added until the completed item is produced.

It is much more like trying to sort out a box of jigsaw puzzle pieces hoping they will come together and create a picture that at some point makes sense.

Number 7 — Can we "lose our eyes" to the grief roller coaster and avoid the emotional ups and downs of the ride? Like the fair ground ride, it still must take place. However, there is support available through groups, unconditionally supportive individuals and help lines, books etc. For me a favourite scripture to help one face a new day, found in St Johns gospel chapter 14 verse 27 where the Master Jesus says –

Peace I leave with you, my peace I give unto you: not as the world giveth, give I unto you. Let not your heart be troubled, neither let it be afraid.

We cannot avoid the roller coaster of life with all its up's and downs. Neither can we avoid the emotional coaster of grief whilst accepting, just as people have their own way of dealing with the fairground roller coaster ride, those facing sudden or prolonged grief will have their own unique experience.

Remember it is your roller coaster you are riding. How you express your grief could be linked to how you deal with life as a whole.

Think for a moment. Have you ever watched folks on a roller coaster? Some are hanging on as instructed, appear to be relaxed and calm throughout the ride. Others will have a look of terror as they face the first sudden swoop down. Then there are those that are hanging on to their rail and scream throughout the whole ride.

Just like the physical roller coaster ride with the different reactions, so is everyone's grief ride.

For some, they will overtly verbalise their emotional responses.

THE ROCKY ROAD OF GRIEF

Others will keep their grief quietly within themself.

Make sure as you ride your grief roller coaster that you journey as is best to bring about healing and hope for the road ahead.

"We bereaved are not alone. We belong to the largest company in all the world – the company of those who have known suffering."

-Helen Keller

CHAPTER 7
GRIEF AND PHYSICAL HEALTH

Grief doesn't just affect our emotions but can have an impact on physical health.

The two go hand in hand and the physical response to grief can be devastating if we do not look after or are unaware of how to support the body structure during what is, a very difficult time.

You may have been very healthy and fit until you alight the grief train.

Suddenly symptoms arise out of nowhere as you bravely struggle on, maybe suppressing those emotions and outwardly are "fine".

It was four years since my husband transitioned heavenward after a long and difficult Alzheimer's journey. Busy writing books, supporting my Care Home family and being a very willing volunteer at my local church, suddenly bizarre health symptoms arose.

As I write this chapter, I am emerging from a year of a healing journey involving a life review and rebalancing my overall day to day living incorporating dedicated relaxation and genuine "sabbath rest" during each week.

If, like me, you are a natural "giver" and love helping others, self-care during your grief onslaught and new way of life, is crucial but understandably difficult.

So how does grief impact our physical health and wellbeing?

When grief confronts us, the physical body will release large amounts of stress hormones which can have an impact on different aspects of the body systems and organs.

As you are trying to adapt to a totally different way of day-to-day living, the body systems are doing their very best to balance the necessary chemicals and hormones for optimal health.

It is known that stress is the major underlying cause of disease. So, how do we define stress?

Stress can be defined as a state of worry or mental tension caused by a difficult situation. Stress is a natural human response that prompts us to address challenges and threats in our lives.

Another description of stress is –

Stress is the body's reaction to harmful situations -- whether they're real or perceived. When you feel threatened, a chemical reaction occurs in your body that allows you to act in a way to prevent injury. This reaction is known as "fight-or-flight" or the stress response.

Grief is a very difficult situation that must be faced, which can easily take toll on the physical body.

This can manifest as time passes and the adjustment journey continues.

Grief stress can affect the body's immune system as the body tries to cope with the new way of life. This can lead to increase of respiratory symptoms, fatigue, loss or increase of appetite.

Craving of sugary carbohydrate foods messes up blood sugar levels in the blood for example.

Grabbing quick processed foods will decrease key nutrients that are essential during times of stress.

Constipation or diarrhea are common results of upsetting the body's usual gut pattern.

Our digestive system is absolutely key to our physical health. It digests our food and absorbs the necessary elements into the blood stream which are then transported to every cell in our body. If you are not looking after your gut health, then sickness creeps in.

In our gut are millions of essential bacteria that influence food digestion. Stress linked with poor eating habits will impact on the levels of gut bacteria which could lead to irritable bowel syndrome suddenly manifesting.

Abnormal stress levels that produce an overload of certain chemicals can produce inflammation anywhere in the body – the joints. muscles, skin e.g.. Brain fog is another symptom of grief or memory loss. It does not mean you are on the dementia pathway.

You may have been a fit and healthy individual until you come face to face with any major loss, then suddenly symptoms pop up and take you by surprise. This is because your normal body rhythm is thrown into disarray.

Grief and chronic stress can also manifest with symptoms such as -
- Headaches
- Muscle stiffness around joints with muscular tension building up in the neck and back region

- Soreness in joints
- Palpitations
- Breathlessness
- Constipation or Diarrhea

Grief and the high level of stress can create inflammation within the body as the immune system battles against the imbalance of chemicals and hormones.

So how should you support your physical body during times of grief and major stress?

Our physical body is made up of around 30 trillion cells that all need nourishment to function optimally to keep us healthy.

Cells make up organs and organs group into specific functional systems. These systems support each other to maintain our overall physical health.

Our blood carries all the essential nutrients, chemicals and hormones to those trillions of cells.

So, one of the key systems to take care of is the ***Digestive System*** where ingested food is digested and the nutrients then absorbed and transported via the blood stream.

When grieving, our body systems are strained to function in full balance and key nutrients struggle to support the body as it goes through the emotional roller coaster of grief.

It is easy to consume those sugary, instant snacks when your body requires a nutritious and health supporting diet.

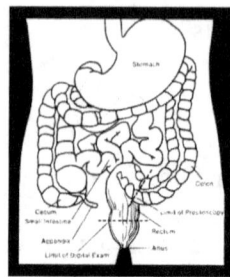

It is said that we are what we eat and assimilate!

There is excellent nutrition information on the internet.

Along with an intake of health supporting foods, it is essential that we are **well hydrated**. Our bodies are composed of at least 80% water, so it is important to drink plenty of water every day.

Next, is **getting enough rest**. Sleep can evade us as we go through emotional turmoil. If night-time, rest of 7-8 hours' sleep is a struggle, short naps during the day can help. Relaxing with calming music, reducing the intake of caffeinated drinks will help.

Exercise is great way to alleviate stress – even a short walk out in the fresh air daily is great. Even walking around the home with windows open can help.

Unconditional Support will assist the journey being taken as grief symptoms arise. Either a support group or someone who can be trusted to listen without "fixing" you.

The physical body often takes a battering during times of grief.

It can manifest even a number of years following the event as the struggle to adjust to the new way of living is taking place.

Take good care of the wonderful body we have been given to minimise any reaction to the grief experience.

"Let thy food be thy medicine and thy medicine be thy food."
– Hippocrates

CHAPTER 8

HOW LONG SHOULD WE GRIEVE FOR?

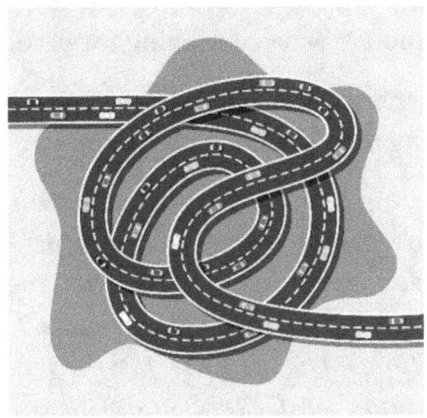

I remember an answer my mother would give if there was no conclusive outcome to a question. It was *"How long is piece of string?"*

On the somewhat unpredictable winding road of grief, is a great answer that we are about to discuss in this chapter.

Knowing that everyone's grief journey is unique to them, it is impossible to conclusively say when the grief journey will end.

Pre – grief experiences can have an impact on the way each individual tackles the twists and turns within the journey of a new way of living and moving forward.

Any life challenge involving grief response can impact on future life e.g. divorce can affect trust in a new relationship; redundancy has the potential to knock one's confidence in securing new employment. Self-esteem may plummet and influence a marriage.

When someone dear dies, a major gap, and the pain of loss takes over.

Imagine being married or with a partner for many years up to 70 plus is devastating for the one left grieving.

Different grieving situations have their own unique expressions resulting in distinctive ways of moving forward.

Here is a statement from American Cancer Society online regrading grieving the death of a loved one –

> *Many people think of grief as a single instance or as a short time of pain or sadness in response to a loss – like the tears shed at a loved one's funeral. But grieving includes the entire emotional process of coping with a loss, and it can last a long time. The process involves many different emotions, actions, and expressions, all of which help a person come to terms with the loss of a loved one. For some people, grief goes on for a long time and seems to not lessen*

So, what is a long time?

We often hear of getting through the first-year anniversaries as if once that's done a magic wand waves and suddenly life progresses "normally".

That is not so. The reality is that the ongoing winding road of adjustment will suddenly resurrect bizarre emotions out of nowhere without any warning.

I recall attending a funeral with my late husband around twenty plus years since my father died. As the coffin was brought into the church, one of daddy's favourite Irish songs started playing – "Oh Danny Boy the pipes are calling…" Immediately memories came flooding back and I found myself quietly sobbing!

I am sure you may have memories of grief moments randomly turning up when a song is played or you attend someone's funeral and are taken back with a jolt to the death of that special person.

Another statement from the online American Cancer Society says –

> It's common for the grief process to take a year or longer. Grief most often gets less intense over time, but the sense of loss can last for decades. Certain events, mementos or memories can bring back strong emotions, that usually last for a short time.

Here it mentions that grief can last for decades.

I recall visiting an elderly gentleman in a Care Home who was deeply distressed following his wife's death some time back. She did everything within their marriage so that he did not even know how to write a cheque.

Maybe the person you are grieving played a significant role of day-to-day responsibilities and suddenly you are left to handle it all.

There is no way that "after the first year" sudden adjustment is going to immediately kick in.

So it is clear that there are so many influences to the way each person's road maps out.

Yes there will be those that quickly start to move forward after loss and those that take years to sort out how they will adjust to the new road ahead of them.

How long should we grieve for could also be phrased "When should I begin grieving?"

Some folks will immediately express their grief and others will wind along the grief road for maybe years before they can deal with their grief.

Others who are caring for someone with a chronic condition could have what is known as anticipatory grief as they prepare themselves, or try to, before that final loss takes place.

Dealing with grief will also be impacted by how everyday life challenges are faced up to. Although loss and grief are linked to someone who has been a very intimate part of life, dying is a new and very unknown territory that is to be navigated.

Unconditional support is key to aiding someone on their new journey. Especially when their grief may suddenly loom up after many years have passed.

It seems clear that there is no definitive answer to how long one should grieve for.

A "grief burst can suddenly pop up and "make you jump" just like the jack in a box!

THE ROCKY ROAD OF GRIEF

Grief response is very much linked to the grieving person's overall makeup and life coping skills.

There is no textbook recipe for grieving. This will challenge those that like to put all life experiences into a logical box.

One might say that life is not a logical journey. How often do sudden unexpected situations crop up that need dealing with?

In closing – grief is not timeline related but the unknown winding road to be navigated as best as possible without judgement or specific expectations.

The reality is that you will grieve forever. You will not 'get over' the loss of a loved one; you will learn to live with it. You will heal and you will rebuild yourself around the loss you have suffered. You will be whole again but you will never be the same. Nor should you be the same nor would you want to.

—Elisabeth Kubler Ross

CHAPTER 9
GRIEF AND DREAMS

How often do you dream?

Do you recall your dreams?

Do you Dream in full colour?

Are you a participant in your dream or an observer?

Experts tell us that we all dream every night but will not necessarily recall them.

Why do we dream?

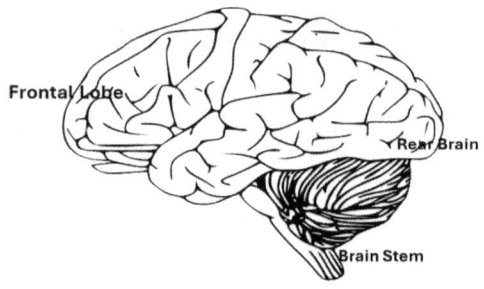

There are not any tangible answers to this question – why we dream or where they originate from.

There are different stages of sleep. One of them is called REM where there is rapid eye movement. In this sleep state the brain stem generates this sleep state while the frontal lobe creates dreams. It is not fully known from a physiological standpoint what constitutes a dream. It could be from imagination or circumstances we experience. Those suffering with PTSD (Post Traumatic Stress Disorder) have nightmares that occur for years following the event.

The fact is that whatever our situation we will all dream. REM sleep and dreams help us process emotions and reduce the impact of them.

There are those that interpret dreams, for example, in the bible in the Old Testament both Joseph and Daniel are famous for their gift of dream interpretation.

There are many to be found on the world wide web who offer dream interpretation. I am sure those that seek answers are relying on them being told positive results!

Dreams are another facet of life experience that help us unravel and deal with various situations occurring throughout our earthly journey.

I actually dream in vivid colour as a main participant. Some are so bizarre that they seem to make no sense at all. Others have to be laughed at when I consider the content.

If daily challenges are spinning around in the mind – our brain overactive when we tuck down – it is possible to have a dream that tries to put things in perspective for the brain to then store.

Different forms of dreams that can be considered–

- General life dreams such as looking for something, but you can't find it or trying to get somewhere or climb a mountain and the end always moves further away.
- About someone deceased but they passed some time ago that may remind you of the last words before they passed or regret that you were not able to get to them before they died.
- A current passing of someone dear to you, either human or a pet.

So, what about dreams in relation to the grief journey? Particularly following the death of someone close to you – a partner, parent, best friend, child or pet.

A gentleman named Dr Joshua Black carried out a 216-participant study of grief and dreams following the death of his father and his own ensuing grief.

The results showed that most dreamers who were grieving found them to be positive and helpful. Only a small minority had negative dreams.

Dreams can have a major impact on healing when you are grieving.

Some people have dreams almost immediately following the death of that special person or pet.

Others will not have dreams they recall for some time, even years hence.

My mother passed to heaven suddenly over thirty years ago and recently (2023). I had more than one very clear dream where she was looking healthy and around her forties. I had not been thinking or talking about her. I had grieved bitterly when she left this earth as there was no time for closure, no time to remind her how much I valued her and loved her. Could God have allowed her be part of a dream to comfort and reassure me following the passing of my lovely husband?

Another dream I recall is where I was with my husband and as I went to talk with him, he turned and walked away. Was that dream of raw grief closure to help me fully let him be free?

You may be reminded of your own dreams of a deceased loved one or pet as you read. Was it telling you anything?

Writing dreams down is a great tool and then, if you are a follower of Jesus, asking the Holy Spirit to show you what the dream means for you.

Some people keep a dream diary. Not a bad idea when we are told that we "work things out" in our dreams.

Writing them down releases things emotionally and can then make some sense from the really bizarre ones.

If there seems to be a recurring pattern to your dreams, something may be lurking within, that needs to be dealt with. For example, forgiveness or releasing guilt associated with the now deceased. Even with a pet there may be guilt around how you came to the decision it was time to let them go.

During the COVID pandemic many people died in care or in hospital without you being present at their last breath. Emotions around this may manifest through dreams to assist with ongoing healing from acute grief emotions.

There is a need for those grieving to grasp the significance and power of dreams to assist with re-adjustment to a new way of walking out life's journey.

I would add that we should take note of the role of dreams in all areas of life.

A final personal story relating to that as someone who believes that God can speak through our dreams.

I had been thinking about whether or not to part exchange my current Peugeot car. I had a dream one night and very clearly, I saw a red car and a clear, strong voice cried out "Red Fiat". A make I had never contemplated buying in all my driving years. The voice was so powerful I decided to follow through what was said to me. Guess what? –

A local Fiat dealership had on their website a Red Fiat at pre-registration price. I followed through and purchased the new vehicle and saved over £8000!!

Never underestimate the power of your dreams to communicate to you and with grief to facilitate with the healing journey.

Why not treat yourself to a grief journal with a cover image that attracts you?

You may want to have a picture of the one you are grieving tucked inside the cover or even on the front cover.

Make it very personal to you as you may want to refer to it as time passes and be proud of how you have adjusted to the new way of living.

If you are someone who does not recall your dreams you can still create a journal and write out poignant moments to release those grief emotions.

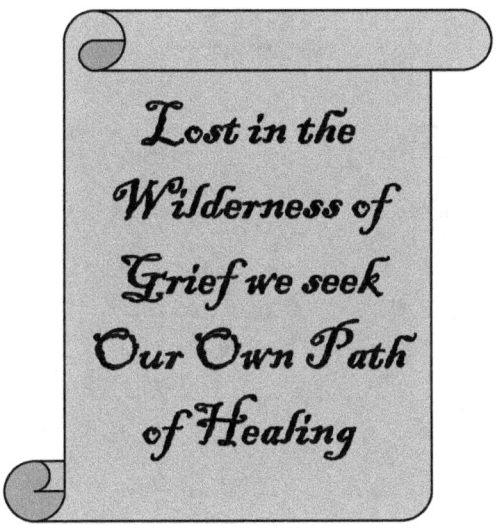

Lost in the Wilderness of Grief we seek Our Own Path of Healing

CHAPTER 10
FINDING A PURPOSE AMONGST THE GRIEF

What do we understand about the phrase "finding a Purpose"?

Merriam Websters dictionary states that the word purpose means something set up as an object or end to be attained: INTENTION or to propose as an aim to oneself.

One could say that finding a purpose from grief is associated with an inner aim to generate something good from all the pains you have suffered

There are many charities and organisations around the world that were born out of tragedy.

Save The Children charity is just one of many charities born out of tragedy at the end of World War ll.

The UK **Marie Curie** End of Life nursing care and support is another example of tragedy to Purpose story.

Smaller charities have been set up following a devastating experience in someone's life as a way to express their grief through concern for others going through the same or similar experiences.

Grief of any kind – death of a spouse, child, pet; loss of a job, sudden illness, divorce, results of a tragic accident etc – changes life for the future drastically.

You lose sight of who you are. Wondering how you will ever adjust to the unexpected, unprepared for road that lies ahead.

The first step to finding your purpose within this new way of life is to -

- Have Compassion on yourself as you navigate this new pathway.
- Know that the way to finding a purpose within your grief is to acknowledge your own grief, seek ways to help you express your grief.
- Accept that the way forward will have its ups and downs and be hard at times just like it was before in life situations.

As you begin to surface from the initial shock and numbness, think of ways that you can help others through your own experience.

Many a person has become very creative as they reflect on their grief journey.

I never expected to be writing the Rocky Road series of books including this one.

Many years ago, when I was sharing with colleagues what were almost amusing nursing experiences I was told "You should write a book!" My response was always "Me! Write a book! Don't be silly!". Were they prophesying my future years hence?

Never underestimate what amazing gift to humanity could arise from your own grief. It may not be world famous, even showing those around – family and friends – how you conquered your challenges, there is nothing more powerful for someone suffering to find comfort and reassurance from someone who "has been there". Giving them confidence to find their way through the grief trial they are going through. Help them work through their own emotions. Just knowing that there is someone who "gets it" and doesn't try to "fix" them.

I found that one of the key things I could share from my own grief journey was the power of prayer – calling out to God and Jesus. It has been a joy to help people realise that the one person who understands suffering and grief is Jesus Christ who suffered terribly and grieved throughout his earthly life. When his friend Lazarus died the shortest bible verse tells us "Jesus Wept".

How do you want to manage your grief walk?

Stay locked in the depths of it

Or walk through it and find a way to turn all the pain into a gift to help others?

THE ROCKY ROAD OF GRIEF

It takes courage to turn pain into purpose, but the upside is that you learn to create a powerful seed to sow that brings joy as you help others climb the stairway of grief.

Finding a purpose through your grief does not mean that you will not have your own grief bumps to navigate when situations can trigger pain again. But you will handle them in a more positive way. What a great tool to share with others so that they too can navigate the ongoing pathway of their life.

Honesty is very important when helping others as they grieve. They will value you and trust your support, knowing that you have been authentic and not tried to brush over the harsh reality of walking alongside grief.

Finding a purpose in life is key to inner joy and peace.

It does not have to be world renowned. For some raising a family is their purpose. For others it can be career focused.

Within turning pain into purpose, it will have its own challenges but the rewards way override the challenges.

As I have been writing the Rocky Road series to help others, memories of my own pain have risen up but have been worth it overall.

I recall going for a hair appointment at the local college and in conversation was able to empathise with the tutor as she faced the challenges with a family member suffering with Dementia.

A purpose may be being open and willing to offer empathy to someone going through what you have been through – or still are facing.

Remember that old saying? "A problem shared is a problem halved"?

So, vow to turn any grief experiences into a purpose!

> If you want to find your purpose in life-
>
> Find your wound
>
> -Rick Warren

CHAPTER 11
COMFORTING WORDS FOR THE GRIEVING HEART

Grief hurts and a grieving heart needs comfort as the new life walk takes place.

The Bible has many comforting words to offer within it that can be used as a comfort while you navigate the grief journey.

If anyone suffered intense grief and torture it was Jesus Christ when he was going to be crucified for the sake of humanity so that mankind could be reconnected with God.

As we have seen through this book, it is OK and important to express our grief

Grief and mourning are spoken about all through the bible offering comfort and hope. The psalmist David was not shy of crying out to God for help in times of grief.

Take comfort from these scriptures –

Job 5:11 The lowly he sets on high, and those who mourn are lifted to safety.

Isaiah 41:10 Don't be afraid, for I am with you. Don't be discouraged, for I am your God. I will strengthen you and help you. I will hold you up with my victorious right hand.

2 Corinthians 1:3 Praise be to the God and Father of our Lord Jesus Christ, the Father of compassion and the God of all comfort, who comforts us in all our troubles, so that we can comfort those in any trouble with the comfort we ourselves receive from God.

Hebrews 13:5 I will never leave you or forsake you

Psalm 73:26 My flesh and my heart may fail, but God is the strength of my heart and my portion forever.

Psalm 34:18 The LORD is close to the broken-hearted and saves those who are crushed in spirit.

Matthew 5:4 Blessed are those who mourn, for they will be comforted.

John 14:27 Peace I leave with you; my peace I give to you. Not as the world gives do I give to you. Let not your hearts be troubled, neither let them be afraid.

Psalm 46:1 God is our refuge and strength, A very present help in trouble

There are many more verses of scripture to help us – to comfort, encourage, uplift and console.

My two favourites from the list above are –

John 14:27 Peace I leave with you; my peace I give to you. Not as the world gives do I give to you. Let not your hearts be troubled, neither let them be afraid.

Psalm 46:1 God is our refuge and strength, A very present help in trouble.

Pick your favourite/s and console yourself by saying them on waking and before going to sleep.

John 14;27 kept me going throughout the pain of the Alzheimer's journey.

Don't be afraid of crying out to God – he hears us and wants to help and support in any time of trouble.

Finally a quote from C.S.Lewis (29 November 1898 – 22 November 1963) who was a British writer, literary scholar, and Anglican lay theologian.

Grief is like a long valley, a winding valley where any bend may reveal a totally new landscape.

RESOURCES

Connect with Sylvia via her website –

https://dementia-whisperer.com/sylvias-opt-in

Find more about "The Rocky Road" book series and other publications –

https://dementia-whisperer.com/publications

Connect via Linked In –

https://www.linkedin.com/in/dementia-whisperer/

Sylvia's Facebook page -

facebook.com/103605086082318

https://dementia-whisperer.com/publications

www.ingramcontent.com/pod-product-compliance
Lightning Source LLC
LaVergne TN
LVHW020435080526
838202LV00055B/5188